D0853077

The HOLIDAYS?? HELP!

Published by Sellers Publishing, Inc.
Text and illustrations copyright © 2011 Sandy Gingras
All rights reserved.

Sellers Publishing, Inc.
161 John Roberts Road, South Portland, Maine 04106
Visit our Web site: www.sellerspublishing.com
E-mail: rsp@rsvp.com

ISBN 13: 978-1-4162-0650-7

10 9 8 7 6 5 4 3 2 1

Printed and bound in China.

The HOLIDAYS?? HELP!

I forgot what they're all about...

by Sandy Gingras

We all know we're not supposed to stress about the holidays, but we do it anyway. We get caught up in cooking the juiciest turkey, finding the most perfect gift, urging our dysfunctional families to function.

We set ourselves up every year, and, every year, we drive ourselves a little crazy with our expectations.

Each year I tell my family, "I'd like to run away for the holidays." I think longingly of swaying in a hammock on a white sandy beach while a steel band plays (not Christmas carols) and nobody bothers me. But then I think, no, because I would miss pumpkins with their toothy carved faces. I would miss the scent of the pine tree. I would miss my crazy imperfect family.

So I stay.

And I try to remember a few things as the holidays approach. They're simple things--moments and memories and emotions that sometimes get ignored or stampeded in the rush of the holidays.

But I know in my heart that they're the things that really count:

hold on

to each other

dance at
the holiday
parties

at The TabLe

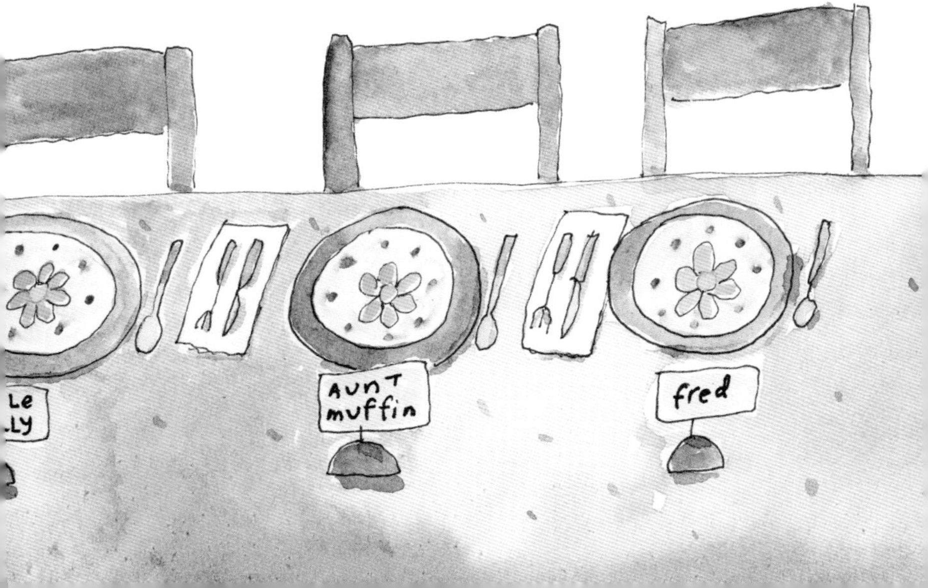

Pause when snow falls quietly in the woods, and catch a snowflake

on your tongue

put extra
marshmallows
in the hot
chocolate

Have ridiculous family
rituals that mean
nothing but are
infinitely precious

Welcome to the Wilber's annual turkey bowling contest!
nice pilgrim outfit
Thanks. you too...

unplug

Follow the old recipes

Grandma's Cookies

1 c. sugar
2 eggs
1 tsp vanilla
2 c. flour
1 c. brown sugar
1 c chocolate chips

Gather together
Stir the memories
Add some love
Lick the bowl

Eat with happiness

Light a
candle

Sing holiday songs and pretend

you know the words (La La humminyhum).

Celebrate
homemade--
bring out the
noodle wreath
your child made
in kindergarten, and
the construction paper
garland too!

Remember that "present" is more about being than buying.

find coziness under
an old quilt

Cook up something
sweet

caLL

home

pick out the
Charlie Brown-iest
tree

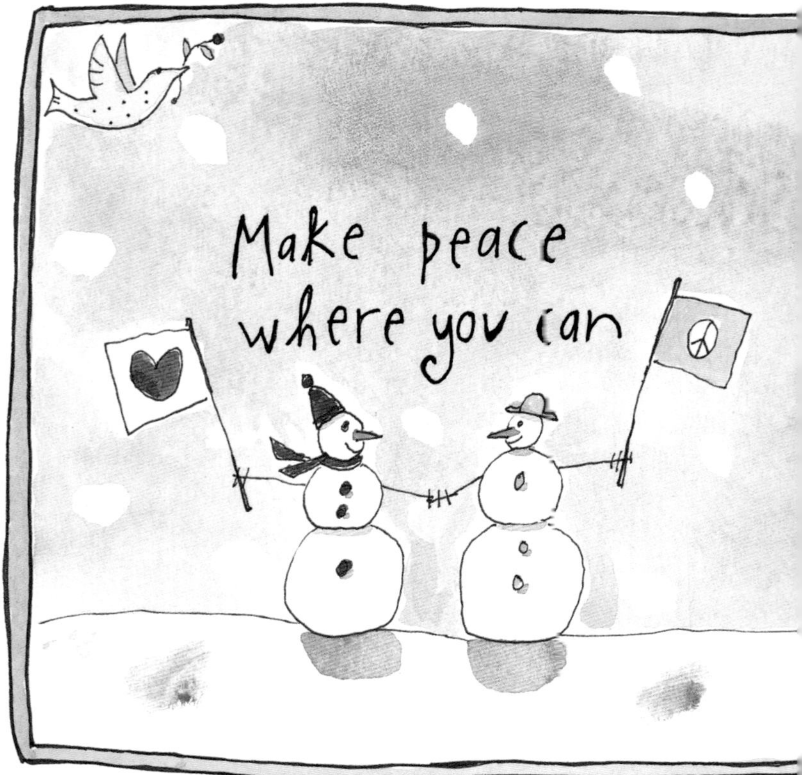
Make peace
where you can

(every Little
bit helps).

KISS UNDER THE MISTLETOE

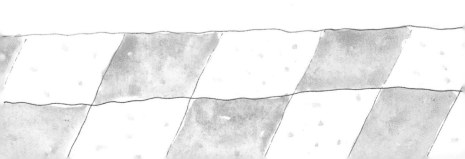

string Lights

in dark pLaces

Make a list of what you already have and be thankful

Carrots for reindeer

Cookies for Santa

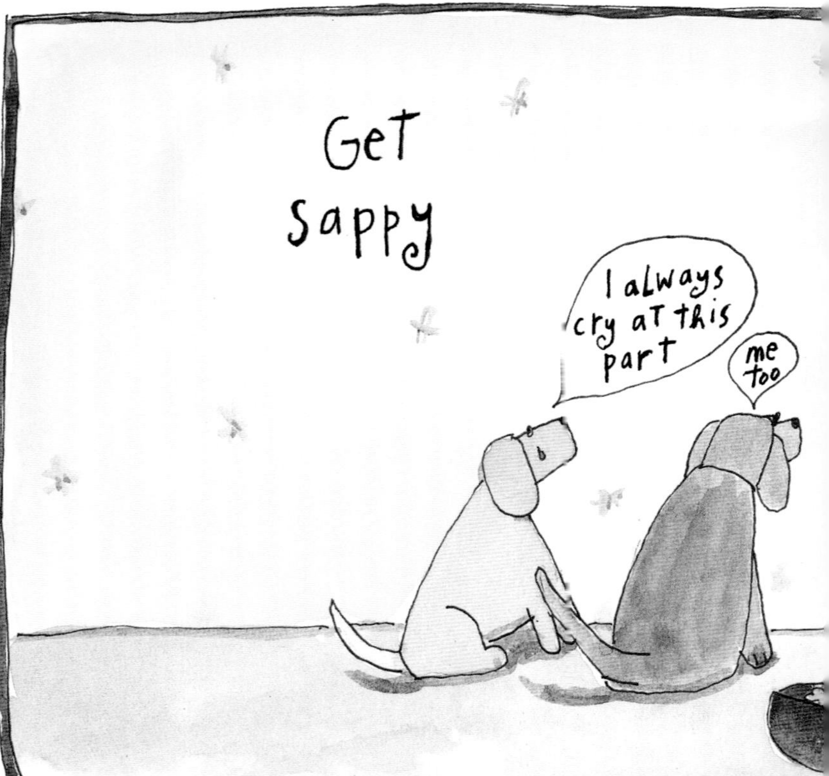
Get sappy
I always cry at this part
me too

open your heart
(it's the greatest
gift of all).

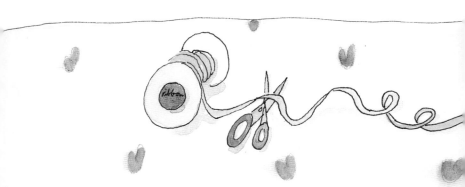

more in the
New Year
(because the world could
use a little more laughter)
and